W9-BVE-407

skiing

Consultant

Cyrus F. Smythe, professor
University of Minnesota
Minneapolis, Minn.

Certified Professional Ski
Instructor

published by:

The Athletic Institute

200 Castlewood Drive
North Palm Beach, Florida 33408

*A not-for-profit organization
devoted to the advancement of
athletics, physical education
and recreation*

Robert G. Bluth, editor

**Library of Congress
Catalog Card Number 79-109498**

**"Sports Techniques" Series
SBN 87670-041-5**

*Published by The Athletic Institute
200 Castlewood Drive
North Palm Beach, Florida 33408*

Foreword

The **"Sports Techniques" Series** is a comprehensive set of instructional aids in sports which are made available by The Athletic Institute. This book is part of a master plan which seeks to make the benefits of athletics, physical education and recreation available to everyone.

The Athletic Institute, a not-for-profit organization devoted to the advancement of athletics, physical education and recreation, believes that sports participation by young and old has benefits of inestimable value to the individual.

The nature and scope of the many Institute programs are determined by nationally-known professional educators who are noted for their outstanding knowledge and expertise in their fields.

The Institute believes that through this book the reader will become more proficient and skilled in the fundamentals of this fine sport. Knowledge and the practice necessary to mold knowledge into playing ability are the keys to real enjoyment in playing any game or sport.

Donald E. Bushore
Executive Director
The Athletic Institute

Introduction

There are few "naturals" in any sport. Skiing is no exception. Learning to ski, like learning any sport, means acquiring *knowledge* of some fundamentals and *practice*. Beginners, whether their physical co-ordination is above or below average, tend to acquire bad habits. The reason is simple. *Natural instincts* generally result in movements which are less efficient than the movements which coaches through long study have developed for more effective performance.

In addition, skiing and some other sports have a further complicating factor which can hamper progress—*fear*. The beginning skier, the beginning horseback rider or swimmer realizes that some physical danger is involved. The desire to minimize the perceived danger increases reliance on the natural instincts. The result is less-than-effective performance. These erroneous natural instincts will be identified throughout the book in addition to those fundamentals which need to be learned for proficiency and enjoyment.

This book is not designed to make one a complete skier. Rather the basic movements needed to control speed and direction with the skis parallel are emphasized. Beyond this level, the skier can read about and experiment with the various techniques constituting the Austrian, American, French or other schools of thought, learn to ski steep slopes in icy or powdery conditions and try highly specialized techniques constantly being developed by racers.

The purpose of skiing is enjoyment. For most individuals, greater skill at a sport leads to greater pleasure. A beginning skier may progress to the highest skill level which age, physical condition, frequency of participation, and boldness will allow.

—Cy Smythe

Table of Contents

the beginning
Equipment 8
The Three Phases of Skiing 10
Instincts vs. Learned Techniques 13
Basic Skiing Stance 16
Skiing Across the Hill (Traverse) 18

beginning control
Alternative Approaches 21
The Traditional Approach 22
The Snowplow Turn 24
Combining the Traverse and Snowplow
   Turn with Stem Turns 26

preparing for the parallel turn
Edge Control 30
Sideslipping 30
Unweighting 32
Adding Unweighting to the Stem Turn 32
Uphill Christie 35

parallel turns
Leg Action 38
Weight Shift 40
Angulation Change 40
Edge Control 42
Upper Body Balance 42
Use of Poles 44

controlling speed
Parallel Turns with Check 46
Short Swing (Wedeln) 47

parallel to start approach
An Alternative for the Young and/or Physically Gifted.... 50
Making Continuous Turns 52

the graduated length method (GLM)
Direct Parallel GLM Method 56
Wedge-Type GLM Method 58

what is a good skier? 59

more about skiing
Buying Bindings, Boots, Skis, Poles and Clothes 64
Preparing to Ski 66
Caring for Your Skis 68
Carrying Skis and Poles 68
Grasping the Ski Pole Correctly 69
Climbing Up the Hill 70
Changing Directions 72
Getting Up from a Fall 73
Learning to Use a Tow or Lift 74
Adjusting Your Skiing to Varying Conditions and Terrain.. 78
Safety Precautions to Remember 79

glossary of skiing terms 81

the beginning

A beginning skier should rent ski equipment for the first few times to achieve a better understanding of the fit and feel of skis, boots and poles of various sizes and manufacture. He can also make certain that skiing is a sport he wishes to pursue often enough to justify buying equipment.

The beginner should also take skiing lessons from the start. An instructor can help to evaluate the beginner in terms of age, physical condition, aggressiveness and anticipated frequency of ski days. This will enable the newcomer to choose the most effective way to approach the sport. In addition, the novice will avoid developing a host of bad habits which he will need to forget later.

A Special Note Concerning Children—

Parents should not push their children; rather they should make snow fun. Children will learn through imitation, not appeals to intelligence. To perfect ski technique at a young age is not all-important. Youngsters should be given "easygoing" lessons. Above all, the parents must not get emotional. Children will copy good skiers. Let them follow the instructor's movements.

Equipment

Boots:

Ski boots should fit the foot as a glove fits a hand, allowing no excess room. A ski boot is not a shoe. The boot's primary purpose is for skiing, not walking. The skier should buy a snug fit, not a boot which must be laced or buckled tightly for fit and support. Boots are the most important piece of skiing equipment which a beginning skier will purchase. If the boots do not give good support and control with reasonable comfort, the skier will neither enjoy skiing nor progress as quickly as he otherwise might.

Poles:

The lighter the pole, the better. Length should approximate three-quarters of the skier's height.

Skis:

For the beginner, skis should fit a bit shorter and certainly no longer than the skier's height. For the intermediate skier, skis four to six inches taller than his height may be used.

Bindings:

The release binding used should be properly set for the skier's weight and skiing level and maintained according to manufacturer's specifications.

1. **TEST BINDINGS TO MAKE SURE THEY RELEASE PROPERLY.**
2. **ONE QUITE SIMPLE TEST IS TO KICK TOE OF OPPOSITE FOOT IN BINDING WITH FREE FOOT.**

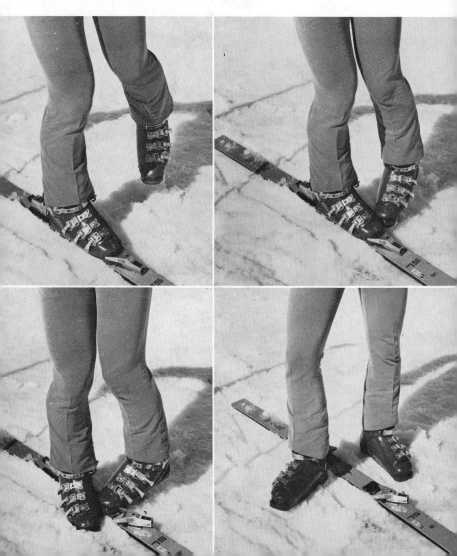

The Three Phases of Skiing Technique

Acceleration

Skiing techniques change constantly and will continue to be modified by what racers do. However, not all of the acceleration and turning techniques which develop from racing are useful to recreational skiers. Racers are young, quick, physically coordinated individuals who in their quest for speed, ski on the fringes of control. The average skier is interested primarily in enjoyment, not mechanical efficiency in attaining speed. The physical condition, the reflex actions and the timing required of an individual in a number of racing maneuvers are far beyond the average skier's abilities. Racers will continue to influence and improve recreational ski technique, but caution must be exercised in adopting the racer's movements to achieve goals which are different from those of a skier interested in control rather than acceleration.

Braking for Control

In mastering braking techniques, the skier is concerned with attaining *control* over *speed and direction*. The instructor's goal is to bring a beginning skier to a level of ability consistent with the newcomer's physical skills, age, frequency of skiing and boldness. This phase finishes when the skier has learned to control *speed* and *direction* on moderate slopes with the skis parallel. The fundamentals learned up to that point permit the skier to move into either of the other two phases of skiing—racing or free skiing. The fundamentals involved at this first level of skiing are:

- **A BALANCED POSITION ON MOVING SKIS**
- **EDGE CONTROL**
- **UNWEIGHTING**
- **TURNING POWER**
- **ECONOMY OF MOTION**
- **WEIGHT TRANSFER**

Free Skiing

Free skiing techniques are a blend of the first level of skiing, the acceleration techniques of the racers and specific techniques developed to add variety to ski turns. The expert skier can use various maneuvers for maximum enjoyment on a variety of snow conditions (ice, packed or powder) and terrain conditions (flat, moderate, steep, bumps.)

Instincts vs. Learned Techniques

What feels right is often wrong in many sports. Skiing is no exception. The beginner, trusting *natural instincts,* quickly acquires bad habits unless he is corrected. Skiing is further complicated by a fear of falling which causes greater reliance on natural instincts than is found in sports where a sense of danger is not felt.

For skiing, natural instincts are exactly wrong. Thus, the beginner who can do the opposite of what he feels is right will be building a foundation for good technique.

Leaning Backward When Going Downhill

When a person walks downhill, he instinctively leans backward. This position is comfortable and gives a secure feeling. Should a person slip and fall, it would be more natural to fall backward against a slope rather than forward and down a slope. Such a position is disastrous for a beginning skier.

DO NOT LEAN BACK

Leaning backward causes the skis to accelerate out from under the skier, and as a result the skier loses control. Skiing requires a balanced position over the skis. The balance point will vary as the skis accelerate and decelerate or as the terrain changes. A racer may find that getting his weight to the back of the skis is useful in accelerating. The beginning skier will generally progress faster and have more control with his weight placed more toward the front of the skis. This is achieved by bending forward at the ankles and keeping the knees flexed.

Leaning Uphill
When Crossing a Hill

As a person walks across a hill, his tendency is to lean uphill, placing more weight on the uphill foot. Instinct tells one that if he falls, the uphill fall is safer and shorter than falling downhill. In skiing, this instinct hampers progress. On skis the skier needs to lean downhill, the extent of which depends upon the

POOR FORM   **DESIRED POSITION**

slope, speed and snow conditions. Leaning downhill is accomplished by bending sideways slightly at the waist, thrusting the knees uphill to keep more weight on the downhill ski rather than the uphill ski. The resulting body position is commonly known as *angulation*. There are a number of body movements in the shoulders, waist and knees which can fine-tune this position to achieve a particular maneuver. For the beginner, the most efficient approach is to bend sideways at the waist so that the body always angles over the downhill ski.

Stiffening When Afraid

The third instinct which hampers the beginning skier is the human tendency to stiffen when afraid. It is natural for a novice skier to feel fear. In fact, even a veteran skier will tend to panic a bit if he suddenly comes upon a patch of ice or a difficult bump. However, this stiffening reaction is wholly undesirable. Learn to relax. Tense muscles cannot react and flex as well as relaxed muscles.

TOO STIFF   **RELAXED AND COMFORTABLE**

Basic Skiing Stance

To begin, pick a gently sloping hill with a flat running area at the bottom upon which you may glide to a stop if necessary. By so doing, you minimize danger to yourself and to others.

Bend the knees and ankles. Boots should never be buckled so firmly that the ankles cannot be flexed forward. This bend in the knees and ankles will help provide balance. The muscles should be relaxed to serve in the same way that springs and shock absorbers in a car absorb the shock of bumps in the road.

Keep the skis flat on the snow and about six to eight inches apart for good balance. Keeping the skis flat upon the snow avoids the loss of control from swerving or turning as a result of an edge biting into the snow. With acceleration, thrust the knees and ankles forward to maintain balance over the skis. Remember, by sitting back the skis will accelerate faster—generally resulting in the fall.

A novice should learn to feel that each ski is a separate unit and can be used independently.

Look ahead and not at the ski tips while bending the waist slightly. One common fault of beginning skiers is to straighten knees and ankles while bending excessively at the waist.

The hands should be ahead of the body at about the waist level. The arms should not be allowed to hang limp nor should the hands be held at the shoulder level.

In slowing down, come back with the knees and ankles to a balanced position on a decelerating ski. An important lesson to learn early in skiing is to be ready with bent knees to go forward or backward with the ankles, knees and hips when accelerating or slowing down.

1. **BEND KNEES AND ANKLES FOR BALANCE.**

2. **KEEP SKIS FLAT UPON SNOW, 6 TO 8 INCHES APART.**

3. **BEND AT WAIST SLIGHTLY AND LOOK AHEAD.**

4. **POSITION HANDS WAIST-HIGH IN FRONT OF BODY.**

5. **ALWAYS BE READY TO MOVE ANKLES, KNEES AND HIPS FORWARD OR BACKWARD WHEN ACCELERATING OR SLOWING DOWN.**

Skiing Across the Hill (Traverse)

The flexed body position used for downhill skiing is also used in *traversing*. The knees and ankles are bent but relaxed. The waist bend is slight, not exaggerated. The back is fairly straight. The skis are comfortably apart for balance.

Note These Differences:

- The uphill ski is advanced ahead of the downhill about two to four inches. This tends to happen without effort.

- More weight is placed on the downhill ski for control of direction and balance.

- The waist should be bent slightly over the downhill ski to assist in maintaining weight over the downhill ski. The resulting body position is called *angulation*.

SKIS TOO FLAT
SLIDING DOWNHILL.

KNEES MOVING TOWARD
DOWNHILL, CAUSING SLIDING.

As you become accustomed to the feel of traversing, use your knees in a different fashion. Push the knees slightly uphill without changing the basic traverse position. You should feel the skis' edges bite more deeply into the snow. Then push the knees slightly downhill until the edges lose their bite. Notice that you slip downhill while going across the hill. Such edge control is vital to skiing. Begin to "play" with the edges as soon as possible.

Traverse Position

1. **ASSUME FLEXED BODY POSITION.**

2. **UPHILL SKI AHEAD OF DOWNHILL SKI, 2 TO 4 INCHES.**

3. **FOR CONTROL, PLACE MOST WEIGHT ON DOWNHILL SKI.**

4. **BEND WAIST SLIGHTLY AND MAINTAIN WEIGHT OVER DOWNHILL SKI.**

beginning control

Alternative Approaches

There are several basic learning approaches to reach the same, primary skiing goal—that of *parallel skiing with speed and direction control.* The alternatives are:

1. **THE TRADITIONAL APPROACH.**

2. **THE PARALLEL TO START METHOD.**

3. **THE GRADUATED LENGTH METHOD (GLM)— WEDGE TYPE**

4. **THE GRADUATED LENGTH METHOD (GLM)— DIRECT PARALLEL**

The choice is dependent on a number of factors: age, physical condition, frequency of skiing, mental attitude and physical boldness.

The traditional approach begins with the most basic control position in skiing—*the snowplow.* This is a security blanket and a confidence-building position—not a way to ski. The skier is then taught to work through a series of maneuvers using the pointing of one ski (stemming) to turn until sufficient skill is acquired to undertake parallel turns.

The alternative approach is to avoid the stem action and begin skiing parallel from the start.

Either method works and can result in a polished skier. Parallel skiing from the start usually requires that the beginner be relatively young, have above-average physical coordination and be in good physical condition. In addition, a fair amount of aggressiveness is needed.

The GLM is a **catalyst** to help both young and old learn to parallel-ski after a few lessons (Direct Parallel approach). Beginners start on short skis which are much easier to maneuver and handle. As the skier's ability to control the skis increases, the length of the skis is increased.

The Traditional Approach

The beginning skier who steps onto a hill in boots which feel overly large; attached to skis which look too long; holding poles which feel awkward, may be a bit apprehensive about the whole thing. As the skis seem to start sliding, the beginner becomes primarily concerned with how to check and control speed. The position traditionally utilized to do this is the *snowplow*. This is the basic control maneuver in skiing. Racers will use it to glide slowly into a lift line or by a gate on a race course to check its position.

Again, the snowplow should be regarded not as a way to ski, but as a combination confidence-builder and good-habit former. As soon as it serves its purpose, you should move on to more comfortable and interesting maneuvers.

The snowplow is easy to learn. Face downhill with the tails of the skis spread wide keeping the tips of the skis about four inches apart. The skis should be nearly flat upon the snow to slide easily. Do not bow knees inward. Rather, legs should be kept straight from hips to feet.

The body position in other respects is the same as for skiing straight downhill. The knees and ankles should be bent for balance and flexibility.

While maintaining this position, slide down a gradual slope absorbing any unevenness in terrain in the ankles and knees and not by bending at the waist. Rock forward and backward at the knees and ankles as the skis accelerate or decelerate to maintain a balanced position over the skis.

To check the speed simply push the tails of skis out farther, keeping the ski tips about four inches apart. The wider the tails are displaced, the slower the speed. To reduce speed further or to stop altogether, roll both knees slightly inward to make the inside edges of the skis bite more firmly into the snow.

1. **SPREAD TAILS OF SKIS WIDE AND KEEP TIPS ABOUT 4 INCHES APART.**

2. **SKIS NEARLY FLAT UPON SNOW.**

3. **KEEP LEGS STRAIGHT FROM HIPS TO FEET. DON'T BOW KNEES.**

4. **BEND KNEES AND ANKLES FOR BALANCE AND FLEXIBILITY.**

Common Snowplow Errors:

- Riding the inside edges of the skis with the knees excessively bent inward. Women especially seem prone to this bad habit. The skis tend to cross, resulting in a rather panic-provoking situation.

- Straight knees and ankles with excessive waist bend.

- Keeping the tails of the skis too close together to maintain a slow descent.

The Snowplow Turn

Changing direction in a snowplow is easily accomplished. Merely shift weight to one ski while maintaining the position of the skis.

Learning to turn, however, is not nearly as important as *learning to utilize movements which can prepare you for more advanced skiing.* A beginning skier can turn easily in the snowplow with weight transfer, which creates a possibility of learning bad habits. Therefore, shift weight with *two definite movements.*

1. Lean out over the more heavily weighted ski at the waist. The resulting body position is known as angulation.

2. Push the knee slightly inward over the downhill ski causing ski's uphill edge to bite more firmly into the snow. The opposite knee must not bend inward. The relatively less-weighted uphill ski should be kept flat upon the snow.

These two movements will result in a properly angulated position over the weighted ski—a position common to all types of turns at all levels of skiing, including racing. Practice to learn this position from the beginning.

1. FROM BASIC SNOWPLOW POSITION LEAN OUT OVER MORE HEAVILY WEIGHTED SKI.

Many beginners simply cannot believe that the turn is accomplished so easily. They think something more than a simple weight shift is needed.

Avoid the habit of swinging the arms, upper body or hips to make the turn. These unnecessary movements upset balance and create bad habits for higher level turns.

2. **PUSH KNEE SLIGHTLY INWARD OVER THE DOWNHILL SKI CAUSING SKI'S UPHILL EDGE TO BITE INTO SNOW.**

3. **DO NOT BEND OPPOSITE KNEE.**

4. **KEEP LESS-WEIGHTED, UPHILL SKI FLAT UPON SNOW.**

Combining the Traverse and Snowplow Turn with Stem Turns

After maintaining the technique of making turns by using weight shift with angulation, avoid using the snowplow.

Stem turns use the same movements as those used in executing a snowplow turn. The turns start from a traverse and end in a traverse. (Please review the traverse position noted previously.) From a traverse position, point the uphill ski, which is relatively unweighted, slightly downhill. This action is called a *stem.* The stem action is accomplished by pushing the tail of the unweighted ski uphill. The uphill ski now points in the desired direction of travel. To make a turn to a new traverse from the "snowplow-like" position, the movements of the snowplow turn are repeated. Push the knee (uphill ski) slightly forward and to the inside, while the uphill ski is weighted through angulation. The arc of the turn is controlled by the amount of knee movement, forward pressure and edge bite. If a sharper turn is desired, emphasize the action of turning the uphill ski.

1. **FROM A TRAVERSE POSITION POINT UPHILL (UNWEIGHTED) SKI SLIGHTLY DOWNHILL.**

2. **PUSH TAIL OF UNWEIGHTED SKI UPHILL.**

3. **UPHILL SKI POINTS IN DESIRED DIRECTION OF TRAVEL.**

4. **FROM SNOWPLOW POSITION, PUSH KNEE (UPHILL SKI) SLIGHTLY FORWARD AND TO THE INSIDE.**

After turning into the desired direction of travel, let the new uphill ski run parallel to the new downhill ski. In perfecting stem turn movements, turn the stemmed ski by turning the foot and leg of the stemmed ski. Steering the weighted ski by turning the legs is basic for advanced skiing. The more familiarity gained with these movements in the early stages, the more rapidly comes skiing success.

Beware of These Common Errors Which Can Result in Bad Habits:

- Failing to maintain weight on the stemmed ski through the turn and the resulting traverse.

- Turning the hips to help the turn. Twisting the hips is not only unnecessary but will result in poor position for the new traverse. In addition it destroys the ability to angulate properly, to use the edge of the steering ski and to use the legs to assist in turning.

- Swinging the upper body or arms around to help with the turn. These actions are unnecessary and also can easily upset balance.

- Straightening the knees and ankles during the turn.

---

5. ARC OF TURN CONTROLLED BY AMOUNT OF KNEE MOVEMENT, FORWARD PRESSURE AND EDGE BITE.

6. LET NEW UPHILL SKI RUN PARALLEL WITH NEW DOWNHILL SKI.
7. PRACTICE MAKING CONTINUOUS STEM TURNS.

28

preparing for the parallel turn

Edge Control

Often the difference between the first five places in a race is the precision with which the racers use edges. For skiers at all levels, *edge control* is the key to precise control.

From the beginning through expert maneuvers, experiment with edges to achieve a greater "feel" for the precision which properly set edges can add to skiing control and enjoyment.

1. KNEE ACTION IS THE FOCUS OF EDGE CONTROL.

Sideslipping

Either traverse without slipping sideways or traverse forward and slip downhill at the same time. Push the knees uphill enough so as not to slip downhill. The result can be checked by stopping at the end of a traverse and looking back at the line of travel. If you do not slip sideways during the traverse, you should see two continuous grooves cut into the snow by the skis' edges.

Alternate thrusting knees uphill and downhill sufficiently to

At one time, when ski boots were fairly low and flexible, the expert used his ankles and knees in lateral movements to set his edges. Now with plastic or plastic-type boots, which to a large extent eliminate lateral ankle movements, edge control is maintained through the knees. Racers and expert skiers use a variety of subtle knee movements to fine-tune the edge bite. For the typical skier working up to the expert level, knee action should be the focus of edge control.

2. SUBTLE KNEE MOVEMENTS FINE-TUNE EDGE BITE.

allow the skis to slide sideways downhill while traversing across the hill. Too much downhill knee thrust will "catch" the downhill edges and cause you to fall over downhill.

Do not change the basic body position by using the knees laterally to sideslip. The angulation created by bending over slightly at the waist in a downhill direction should be maintained. The knees are used only to achieve the alternating "slip, no-slip" sideways action of the skis.

THRUST KNEES UPHILL THEN DOWNHILL TO ALLOW SKIS TO SLIDE SIDEWAYS DOWNHILL.

Unweighting

The significant difference between the expert and the intermediate skier regardless of the type of turn involves lively leg action. The intermediate skier may understand and utilize weight shift and angulation. He also may have reasonable edge control. Yet the expert has an additional skill of using his knees to unweight his skis on the snow. A good number of skiers do parallel turns. Of these, only a small percentage have the necessary leg action to be classified as expert.

There are two methods to achieve an instant where the skis become relatively "weightless." *The upmotion unweighting method*—rise from a position where the knees are bent. At the top of this rise, the skis are unweighted. *The down-motion*

Unweighting Added to Stem

Learn the nature of the knee action required for parallel turns by adding unweighting to the stem turn.

As the uphill ski is stemmed, sink in the knees. Rise but do

unweighting method—sink with the knees quickly. As the knees are bending, the skis are unweighted.

An expert uses either method, depending on what he is trying to accomplish, the terrain and the snow conditions.

To achieve unweighting, the intermediate skier will find the up unweighting method satisfactory on smooth, moderately sloped hills. Up unweighting generally extends longer and requires less precise timing. Therefore, this method gives a greater margin for error than down unweighting.

1. **UNWEIGHTING PROVIDES INSTANT OF "WEIGHTLESSNESS"**

2. **NOTE THE KNEE ACTION OF UP UNWEIGHTING METHOD SHOWN BELOW.**

not straighten the knees as your weight is transferred to the uphill ski. Then bring the downhill ski to parallel the uphill ski. Complete the turn by sinking in the knees to cause the edges to bite more firmly.

1. **STEM UPHILL SKI WITH A SINKING IN BOTH KNEES.**

2. **RISE IN KNEES AND TRANSFER WEIGHT TO UPHILL SKI BY ANGULATING OVER UPHILL SKI.**

To the regular stem turn has been added a down-up-down motion which achieves two purposes. The stem turn now called a *stem christie turn* is easier, more controlled, more precise and more fun. The knee action learned is the kind of action required for executing a proper parallel turn.

You may gain positive control if the up-motion used to bring the downhill ski up to the stemmed ski is not mainly an up-motion but an up and forward in the knees motion. Driving slightly forward with the knees as the skis are brought together helps maintain a balanced position on the accelerating skis.

After becoming familiar with this stem christie turn, gradually reduce the width of the stem until the stem is quite narrow, then substitute for the wider stem a firm turning of the legs and increased edge bite for control.

3. **AFTER BRINGING DOWNHILL SKI UP PARALLEL WITH STEMMED SKI, RISE IN KNEES AND TRANSFER WEIGHT TO UPHILL SKI BY ANGULATING OVER UPHILL SKI. BRING DOWNHILL SKI UP PARALLEL WITH STEMMED SKI.**

4. **SINK IN KNEES TO COMPLETE TURN WHILE INCREASING EDGE BITE OF SKIS BY PUSHING KNEES INWARD AND TURNING FEET AND LEGS.**

5. **RISE INTO NEW TRAVERSE POSITION.**

6. GRADUALLY REDUCE WIDTH OF STEM.

Uphill Christie

As the down-up-down motion added to the stem turn becomes comfortable, begin to use this same leg action to make turns uphill with the skis parallel. Such turns are called *uphill christies.* From a traverse, sink in both knees. Rise but do not straighten the knees, and at the top of this turn the feet and knees slightly uphill. Then sink down with the knees and ankles to finish the turn uphill.

This turn is accomplished easily. The leg action is identical to the required action of downhill parallel turns and stem christie turns.

Do not swing around with the hips, swing the arms or the upper body. These movements are not needed and diminish your ability to progress smoothly into parallel skiing.

Stem christie turns and the uphill christie develop the kind of strong, positive leg action and upper body control essential for advanced skiing. Skiing is done from the waist down, even though natural instincts prompt us to be more active in the upper body to compensate for too little action in the legs.

1. **WEIGHT SHOULD BE ON DOWNHILL SKI THROUGHOUT MANEUVER.**

2. **USE GOOD KNEE ACTION—MORE THAN BELIEVED NECESSARY.**

3. **KEEP UPPER BODY AS MOTIONLESS AS POSSIBLE.**

parallel turns

All of the turns proceeding to the parallel turn have relied on turning power created by changing weight to a stemmed ski pointed in the desired direction of travel. To turn without such stemming action, another turning force must be brought to play.

Leg action utilized in the uphill christie is the heart of the *downhill parallel turn.* This down-up-down motion with the knees and ankles provides a moment during which the skis are relatively unweighted on the snow. During this moment of reduced resistance between skis and snow, the skis can be easily turned to another direction. Without such unweighting, turning the skis is considerably more difficult; moreover, in loose snow it is almost impossible.

Leg Action

For a traverse, sink down in the knees as is done for both the stem christie and uphill christie turns. Do not change the angulation or make any upper body movement. Simply sink in the knees, maintaining the most weight on the downhill ski. Then, with an up-motion of the knees to achieve an instant of unweighting, turn the feet and legs in the desired direction of the turn.

Note:

At this point, a very common problem may arise. Most skiers trying downhill parallel turns for the first time are a bit apprehensive. They think that this turning action of the feet and legs must fully complete the turn into the new traverse. This is not true. This turning action only starts the skis in a new direction. The turn is completed by edge control and a balanced position on the skis which because of their shape complete the turn. Attempting to make the whole turn with one mighty effort of the feet and legs when the skis are unweighted is not only unnecessary but makes the turn jerky and sudden. Also, balance is difficult to maintain. At this level particularly, look for smooth movements and balance to build grace into advanced skiing.

1. SINK IN KNEES MAINTAINING MOST WEIGHT ON DOWNHILL SKI.

2. UP-MOTION OF KNEES ACHIEVES INSTANT OF UNWEIGHTING.

3. TURN FEET AND LEGS IN DESIRED DIRECTION OF TURN.

4. LET EDGE CONTROL AND BODY BALANCE COMPLETE THE TURN.

Weight Shift

The turning of the legs and feet as the skis are unweighted only starts the turn. The unweighting is of short duration.

Following the unweighting, transfer weight from the former downhill ski to what is to be the new downhill ski as the turn is completed. This weight change must be positive and permanent throughout the turn and into the new traverse. Con-

Angulation Change

With the sinking action of the knees, the angulation achieved to start the parallel turn is over the downhill ski. This angulation is released as the skis are unweighted and is established over the newly weighted ski.

tinue to sink in the knees after the unweighting throughout the turn to accomplish the turn more smoothly and with greater control.

1. **FOLLOWING UNWEIGHTING, TRANSFER WEIGHT FROM DOWNHILL SKI TO NEW DOWNHILL SKI.**

2. **WEIGHT CHANGE IS POSITIVE AND PERMANENT THROUGHOUT TURN.**

3. **CONTINUE TO SINK IN KNEES THROUGHOUT TURN.**

1. **TO START PARALLEL TURN, ANGULATE OVER DOWNHILL SKI.**

2. **AFTER SKIS ARE UNWEIGHTED, ANGULATE OVER NEWLY WEIGHTED SKI.**

Edge Control

The edges should be changed along with the change in weight and angulation. To gain additional positive control in the turn, press the knee of the newly weighted ski slightly

Upper Body Balance

While skiing the upper body always should be relaxed and still. Primarily, skiing is done from the waist down. An expert skier gives the appearance of lively leg action with minimum

inward. This inward knee press increases the bite of the turning ski's edge which assists in making the turn.

1. **PRESS KNEE OF NEWLY WEIGHTED SKI SLIGHTLY INWARD.**

2. **KNEE PRESS INCREASES BITE OF TURNING SKI'S EDGE.**

movement above the waist. The upper body acts to counterbalance the action of the lower body.

1. **USE GOOD LEG ACTION WITH MINIMUM MOVEMENT ABOVE WAIST.**

2. **UPPER BODY ACTS TO COUNTERBALANCE ACTION OF LOWER BODY.**

Use of Poles

Learn parallel turns without the use of poles. A tendency while first trying parallel turns is to use the poles to achieve unweighting rather than positive leg action. The result is inadequate leg movement and overactivity of the upper body.

Plant the pole into the snow as the bending action in the knees concludes and the "straightening" action begins to achieve unweighting. Use the pole to assist unweighting.

Planting the pole earlier prevents the continuation of the knees down and limits unweighting. Pushing on the pole as one starts straightening the knees assists the up-movement of the knees more positively and makes the pivoting of the legs and feet easier. In parallel turns:

1. **PLANT POLE WHEN UNWEIGHTING ACTION BEGINS.**

2. **USE POLE TO ASSIST UNWEIGHTING.**

controlling speed

Parallel Turns with Check

Speed control in parallel turns is achieved to a large extent by the *angle of the turn.* After the turn, a new traverse brings the skis into a line running almost straight across the hill and provides for a slow, constant rate of speed. However, if the hill is too steep or narrow to allow much of a traverse, additional speed control may be desirable. On the initial down movement with the knees, bend the knees more than for a normal turn and push the tails of the skis downhill. The skis turn slightly uphill and across the direction of travel. The start of the up-unweighting motion is sharper and sets the edges of the skis into the snow. At the top of the up-unweighting motion, turn the skis with the feet and legs into a new direction to complete the parallel turn.

The turning of the skis uphill and the strong set of the edges will reduce speed.

1. TURN SKIS UPHILL.

2. SET EDGES WITH FIRM UP-MOTION.

3. DO NOT SIT BACK WHILE TURNING SKIS DOWNHILL TO ACCELERATE.

4. POLE ACTION IS NOT A SUBSTITUTE FOR STRONG LEG ACTION.

Short Swing (Wedeln)

Short swing, a term often used interchangeably with the term *Wedeln,* refers to a series of parallel turns straight downhill with no traverse. This maneuver requires rhythm and precise timing of leg and pole action (Refer to "Use of Poles" in parallel turns, page 44).

In short swing, the line of travel is straight downhill while the skis make repeated movements across the direction of travel. The shorter the swing of the skis across the *fall line,* the less the reduction of speed. Wide swings of the skis with a hard setting of the edges reduce speed even on steep hills.

Viewed from above, the impression is that the upper body is quiet—relatively immobile—while the lower body acts to pivot the skis back and forth to keep the speed reduced. The skis sideslip across the fall line as the knees compress.

**1. SHORTER SWING FOR MORE SPEED.
   WIDER SWING FOR LESS SPEED.**

2. **KEEP UPPER BODY MOTIONLESS TO COUNTERBALANCE LEG ACTION.**

3. **DON'T ROCK BACK ONTO HEELS. KEEP A BALANCED POSITION OVER THE CENTER OF SKIS.**

4. **PRACTICE POLE AND LEG-ACTION RHYTHM TO MAKE TURNS MORE SMOOTHLY.**

parallel to start
approach

An Alternative for the Young and/or Physically Gifted

Speed checks may be achieved by beginners without use of the traditional snowplow.

Turn the skis quickly across the direction of travel. In a straight downhill run, the skis are flat upon the snow and about five to six inches apart.

When making the turn, place more weight on the downhill ski. Bend at the waist slightly over the weighted downhill ski. Vary the length of the sideslipping in the turn by lateral movements of the knees. Just prior to the turn, sink in the knees. Then push up with the knees and turn the legs and feet to make the skis turn across the hill. As soon as the turn is completed, sink in the knees while sliding sideways down the hill.

To reduce speed, move legs and feet forcefully to turn the skis across the direction of travel. Sink with the knees to maintain balance and increase the bite of the skis' edges. Turn only the feet and legs; the upper body remains stable, motionless and faces downhill. The turn resembles the hockey player's stop. For short swing turns, pivot the skis under the upper body.

Because skiers are either right-legged or left-legged, speed check turns are made more easily and smoothly one way than the other. Work on the turn both ways and achieve control over both turns.

1. PLACE MORE WEIGHT ON DOWNHILL SKI.
2. BEND AT WAIST SLIGHTLY OVER WEIGHTED DOWNHILL SKI.

3. VARY LENGTH OF SIDESLIPPING IN TURN
   THROUGH LATERAL MOVEMENTS.

4. USE GOOD KNEE ACTION. SINK IN KNEES, THEN PUSH
   UP. TURN LEGS AND FEET TO CONTROL SKIS
   ACROSS HILL.

5. COMPLETE TURN AND SINK IN KNEES TO
   SIDESLIP DOWNHILL.

Making Continuous Turns

Utilizing weight shift with angulation, edge control and the knee action learned in the speed check turn, continue skiing across the hill with as little or as much sideslipping as is comfortable. Make continuous turns by alternating directions. With good knee action use a *down-motion* to prepare, an *up-motion* to turn and a *down-motion* to finish each turn. Transfer weight from ski to ski with each turn. Again, keep the upper body quiet and allow the legs to do the work.

Greater control over the arc of the turn is achieved by pushing the downhill knee inward to increase the bite of the downhill ski's edge into the snow.

This increased bite causes the ski to turn more sharply, thereby reducing speed quickly. Additional control of the arc is developed by continuing to turn the downhill ski leg as the turn is made. Keep feet comfortably apart in learning parallel turns. As experience allows, the feet may be brought together if desired for style.

After acquiring more ability to control both speed and direction on fairly easy slopes, work on the refinements of smooth, parallel skiing.

1. **MAKE CONTINUOUS TURNS BY ALTERNATING DIRECTIONS.**

2. **WITH GOOD KNEE ACTION EXECUTE A DOWN-MOTION TO PREPARE, AN UP-MOTION TO TURN AND A DOWN-MOTION TO FINISH EACH TURN.**

3. **TRANSFER WEIGHT FROM SKI TO SKI, LETTING LEGS DO THE WORK WHILE KEEPING UPPER BODY MOTIONLESS.**

4. **WORK TO REFINE PARALLEL MOVEMENTS ON EASIER HILLS.**

5. **THEN PROCEED ONTO MORE CHALLENGING SLOPES.**

the graduated length method (GLM)

This "method" starts beginning skiers on skis much shorter than usual. The first length for adults may measure slightly more than three feet. As the beginning skier acquires greater control, the length of the skis is increased. Finally, the skier progresses to the length of skis chosen for permanent use.

The prime advantage of the GLM method is that it facilitates learning parallel turns right from the start. In fact, many are able to make parallel turns after the first or second lesson. What a great psychological boost this is to the beginning skier, as well as a practical means to learn skiing techniques faster and better.

A lower accident rate among GLM graduates is not clearly determined. However, in support of such an hypothesis the GLM allows a beginning skier a chance to develop muscles gradually by working up from shorter, lighter skis to longer, heavier ones. A prime contributor to accidents in all sports is fatigue. Also, control over the skis is maintained more easily.

After learning control on short skis, skiers "graduate" to longer skis for greater speed, although for most recreational skiers sufficient speed can be generated on short skis. Longer skis provide the greater braking power needed because of the increased speed. For many, speed is one of skiing's most thrilling aspects. The popularity of ski racing has increased significantly. Yet it is important to ski only as fast as can be controlled. Uncontrolled speed is another prime contributor to skiing accidents.

Direct Parallel GLM Method

The present-day parallel GLM approach is based on swiveling the skis rather than stemming or stepping. All basic techniques apply as presented in the "parallel turns" section beginning on page 37. Through proper application of these

(parallel turn)

1. LOWER BODY TURNING POWER KEY TO PARALLEL TURN.

2. UNWEIGHT BY SINKING IN THE KNEES TO PROVIDE AN INSTANT OF WEIGHTLESSNESS WHEREBY FEET AND SKIS TURN MORE EASILY IN SNOW. PIVOT ON BALLS OF FEET. (WITH MORE EXPERIENCE PIVOTS ON TOES OR HEELS MAY BE ACCOMPLISHED ACCORDING TO TERRAIN AND SNOW CONDITIONS.)

3. TRANSFER WEIGHT TO OUTSIDE SKI FOR BETTER CONTROL. PRESS KNEES TOWARD TURN TO SET EDGE BITE.

4. INSIDE FOOT, KNEE AND HIP LEAD SLIGHTLY THROUGHOUT TURN. UPPER BODY BALANCE LENDS CONTROL AND GRACE TO MAKING TURN.

techniques, the turning action of the skis is achieved more easily due to the shorter length of the skis. Many professional ski instructors prefer to have students learn "stem-action" skills after first learning to parallel-turn. The stemming action is taught as a safety measure for skiing uneven terrain and difficult situations. The key is that GLM students do not first learn the stemming movement, which they later must "un-learn" when advancing to parallel-turn maneuvers.

1. PRACTICE TURNS WITHOUT POLES. PALMS DOWN PROVIDE FOR BETTER BALANCE. PALMS UP INDICATE THAT CENTER OF GRAVITY IS TOO HIGH.
2. UP AND DOWN (OR DOWN AND UP) UNWEIGHTING MOTION ADDS RHYTHM TO SKIING MOVEMENTS AND IMPROVES POSITION OVER SKIS.
3. PIVOT FEET RHYTHMICALLY, KEEPING SKIS FLAT UPON THE SNOW.
4. NOT NECESSARY TO ROTATE OR COUNTER-ROTATE UPPER BODY TO MAKE SMOOTH, POWERFUL TURNS. SLIGHT ROTATION OR COUNTER-ROTATION OF THE SHOULDERS MAY BE INDIVIDUALLY PREFERABLE, HOWEVER.

Wedge-Type GLM Method

Some ski schools prefer to teach a wedge-type GLM method whereby students proceed through more traditional skiing phases. Adult beginners start on skis of four to five feet in length and proceed from snowplow skills to "wide track" parallel turns. The primary advantage of this method is that the student learns balance and control from a variety of positions. Also, progressing from wide-track to closed-stance parallel movements helps develop with control the many approaches from which parallel turns can be made. The Graduated Length Method has greatly accelerated progress through the traditional steps of learning to ski.

1. WEDGE-TYPE GLM SCHOOLS INSTRUCT STUDENTS MORE TRADITIONALLY, PREFERRING TO HAVE STUDENTS LEARN THE SNOWPLOW AND STEMMING ACTION IN PREPARATION FOR PARALLEL SKIING.
2. DIRECT PARALLEL GLM INSTRUCTORS START STUDENTS WITH PARALLEL MOVEMENTS, THEN TEACH THE STEMMING ACTION FOR CONTROL AND SAFETY PURPOSES.

what is a good skier?

Whether you learn speed and direction control the traditional way, the parallel to start approach or GLM, certain fundamentals are important to good skiing.

1. Utilize *lively leg action* with *minimum upper body movement.* Ski with an economy of motion just as the expert in any sport makes key movements which are necessary but give the impression of minimum motion.

2. *Weight transfer* is essential to every ski turn. Timing and smoothness of this weight shift separate the gifted from the ordinary skier.

3. Use *angulation* over the skis as an integral part of skiing. The amount of angulation is finely tuned to the type of turn, the arc of the turn, the snow conditions and the steepness of the hill. For the beginner, angulation is described as a simple leaning out over the weighted ski at the waist. For the expert, angulation is thought of more in terms of edge control, including a variety of movements in the knees, hips, waist and shoulders to achieve desired control over the edges.

4. Maintaining *balance* while learning to parallel ski. Keep your weight slightly forward by bending the knee and ankles. In racing and advanced free skiing, vary your weight forward and backward to achieve balance under a variety of snow, terrain and speed conditions.

5. Gain *experience.* Achieve the ability to control skis under a variety of conditions. Smooth control comes only when the fundamentals are learned and applied under varying snow and terrain conditions.

6. Use *each ski independently*. Normal teaching sequence concentrates on developing edge control of one ski—the uphill edge of the downhill ski. Experts use the edge of either ski to accomplish whatever is desired. The racer learns to use his legs independently. Any advanced skier should start to experiment with these racer actions.

7. Feel free to *experiment* after learning to parallel turn with confidence. From such experimentation come the automatic adjustments required to ski well in the wide range of conditions. Eventually, you will become accomplished enough to employ such advanced techniques as the *Charleston turn,* among others.

The Charleston turn is mentioned because it involves un-orthodox technique. To execute this turn properly, the skier turns on the **uphill** ski.

Once fundamental techniques are mastered, the more un-orthodox techniques may be attempted.

more about skiing

Skiing is a most pleasant pastime for people of all ages who are interested in outdoor activities during winter months.

Basically, skiing falls into four categories: *cross-country,* sometimes referred to as "touring," *downhill,* a basis for competition and recreational skiing; *slalom,* also a basis for competition necessitating skiing agility and speed; *jumping,* one of the more popular international spectator sports.

A ski is a long, narrow piece of wood, metal, plastic or fiberglass so constructed as to have the front portion or "shovel" curved upward and the back portion, referred to as the "heel," squared off. Running lengthwise in the center of the ski is a groove which provides for directional stability. Also specially constructed edges, usually of metal, help the skis "grip" or "bite" into the snow.

A ski designed for jumping is longer, wider and thicker than the conventional recreation ski. The jumping ski has three grooves running lengthwise and no metal edges. The cross-country ski is lighter, thinner and more narrow than the recreation ski.

Buying Bindings, Boots, Skis, Poles and Clothes

Affixed in the middle to the top portion of each ski is a **binding.** Each binding is designed to free the boot from the ski when any unusual stress is applied. This safety feature has prevented many serious injuries.

Be sure to follow the directions accompanying each set of bindings. Some skiers prefer to buy the toe binding of one manufacturer and the heel binding of another. Regardless, make sure you become thoroughly acquainted with the mechanics of your chosen set of bindings before attempting to ski. Your bindings may require adjusting each time you ski. Before skiing always check your bindings by making them release.

Ski boots must be fitted properly to insure maximum safety and control. Purchase boots from dealers who are expert in fitting the foot with the proper boot.

A good ski boot must fit firmly to give the foot and ankle proper support. The boot should "cup" the heel so that it cannot be lifted from the sole. However, the toes should have ample room to allow good circulation. When trying on boots, wear a street sock and a ski sock for the reason that when skiing you may choose to wear two pairs of socks. Incidentally, while skiing, socks are worn inside the ski pants.

There is no exact formula for selecting the **length of your skis.** Most adults choose a length equal to their height plus eight to ten inches. Consult a professional ski instructor or ski equipment dealer when selecting skis, especially when buying skis for children.

A good way to decide the proper **length of your ski poles** is to turn pole upside down so as to grip under the basket while resting the butt of the pole upon the floor. In this position, should your hand be slightly higher than your elbow, the pole is about the correct length.

Ski clothing is designed to keep the skier warm and allow freedom of movement. There are many styles of ski clothing, the choice of which depends upon individual preference. However, in choosing your clothing remember the first layers are most important in keeping you warm. The air trapped between the first layers of clothing and your body acts to insulate you against the cold and wind.

A **good outfit** consists of: thermal underwear, turtleneck undersweater, pants, warm outer-sweater, thermal socks, ski jacket with hood, a cap or protective cover for the head and face, glasses or goggles and a warm pair of gloves. Weather may permit your removing outer layers of clothing. When dressed properly, this may be done easily.

Preparing to Ski

Like most sports, skiing requires physical strength and stamina. Participation in sports such as golf, tennis, basketball, handball, swimming and gymnastics helps you to meet physical-conditioning demands of skiing. Also, a series of selected exercises help to build stamina and physical strength. These exercises include: sit-ups, push-ups, running up stairs, deep knee bends and running in place.

Exercises especially for skiing conditioning are:

Torso Bends, Splits and Twists

Always good as limbering-up exercises for most any sport. Deep knee bends, toe touches with legs straight, jumping jacks, sit-ups and push-ups also serve a useful conditioning purpose.

The following exercises are specifically geared toward toning skiing muscles.

The Chair Exercise

Stand 20 to 40 inches from a wall with your back toward it. Bend your knees until your back rests against the wall with enough pressure to prevent slipping. Support your weight with flexed legs for five minutes.

Knees to Wall Exercise

Stand several inches from the wall while facing it. Keep your heels on the floor and bend your knees to touch the wall. Maintain this position for several minutes.

Foot and Ankle Exercise ("Edging")

Particularly helpful in developing your edge control capability. Begin by transferring your weight from the outside of your feet to the inside from a sitting position.

Repeat the same procedure from a standing position, being careful that you do not strain your ankles. Then take a few steps on the outside of your feet. Take a few more steps on the inside of your feet.

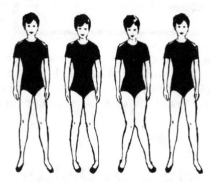

Book Exercise

Try a knee bend with a book placed beneath your toes. This is a particularly good exercise for girls who wear high heels.

Apart from physical conditioning, it's a good idea to practice adjusting your bindings and putting on your skis. Get the feel of how to stand on your skis, how to sit down and how to fall off to the side so as to absorb the shock of the fall with your body. Also, practice rolling over onto your back with your skis on. All of this will help to prepare you for actual skiing.

Caring for Your Skis

Unless your skis are constructed of wood, a coat of lacquer is not required at the beginning of each skiing season.

However, you should become familiar with the types of waxes, one of which you should apply to your skis each day that you ski.

The Three Basic Types of Daily Waxes are:

- Hard paraffin wax for cold temperatures and hard or packed snow.

- Soft paraffin wax for temperatures between 10 and 25 degrees above zero.

- Ultra-soft paraffin wax. For wet snow or temperatures approaching 32 degrees and above.

Rub the waxed surface with a cork to heat the wax and distribute it evenly. As you wax, inspect your skis for gouges or splits. Check the edges to make sure they are in working order. Use a paste wax on the tops of the skis to keep them sealed against moisture.

Carrying Skis and Poles

At first, carrying your skis and poles may seem arduous. But as you become accustomed to handling your ski equipment, the task becomes much easier.

Put skis sole to sole with heels together. Grasp the skis together. Lift the skis to whichever shoulder you prefer. Rest the sides of skis upon your shoulder with shovel end in front. Poles may be carried upon the opposite shoulder and inserted underneath the skis near the heel portion so as to relieve some weight from the shoulder supporting the skis.

Certainly, there are other methods and variations of how to carry your skis and poles. Experiment to find the method most comfortable and best suited for you.

Grasping the Ski Pole Correctly

Use the straps on the ski-pole handles for maximum comfort and support.

Steady the pole with one hand while you slip the opposite hand through the loop.

Grasp the straps and ski-pole grip in the palm of your hand. The loop supports the back of the hand while the tails support the palm.

The straps also provide a safety function should you happen to lose grasp of the pole.

1. **SLIP HAND THROUGH LOOP OF STRAP.**
2. **GRASP TAILS OF STRAP AND HANDLE GRIP WITH PALM OF HAND.**
3. **PROPER GRASP PROVIDES FOR GOOD POLE ACTION.**

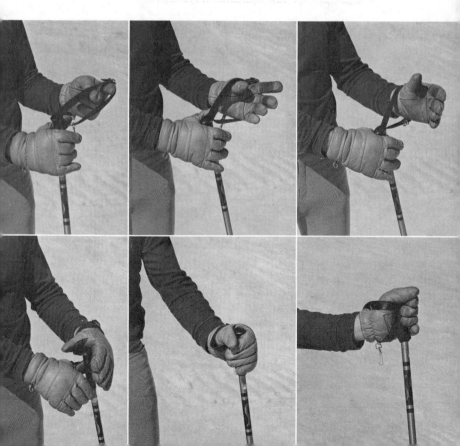

Climbing Up the Hill

Basic to your skiing enjoyment from the time you begin to ski until the time you become rather accomplished at it is the ability to handle your skis with a minimum of effort.

The Sidestep

Particularly effective on steep slopes. It's merely a matter of "stepping" up the hill as you would a flight of stairs while facing sideward. Step off with the uphill ski, then bring the downhill ski up alongside. Repeat this procedure until you reach your destination.

1. **STEP OFF WITH YOUR UPHILL SKI WITH YOUR SKIS AND BODY FACED SIDEWARD TO THE HILL.**

2. **BRING DOWN-SLOPE SKI UP AND ALONGSIDE UPHILL SKI. DIG EDGES INTO SNOW.**

Two useful methods of climbing up a slope when the need arises are the Sidestep and the Herringbone. When you tire of one, simply change to the other.

The Herringbone

On less-steep slopes, this method is usually a faster means to climb.

Place weight over the instep of your feet to dig the inner edges of your skis into the snow. Point tips of skis outward. Lean slightly forward and proceed uphill, alternating your step.

1. **PLACE WEIGHT OVER INSTEP TO BITE INNER EDGES OF SKIS INTO SNOW.**
2. **TIPS POINTED OUTWARD. LEAN SLIGHTLY FORWARD AND ALTERNATE STEPS UPHILL. KEEP POLES OUTSIDE OF "V" FORMED BY SKIS.**

Changing Directions

The kick turn is the basic technique for changing directions.

Bring skis to a parallel position and plant poles near the tips at either end. Face slightly downhill. Swing the tip of your downhill ski forward and up to rest the tail near your uphill foot.

Swivel the raised ski around, using the tail as a pivot point. Place the ski firmly upon the snow and set the uphill edge. Transfer your weight in preparation for swinging the uphill ski around. Bring the ski around to parallel the new uphill ski.

Place your weight over both skis as you set the uphill edges of the skis while using your poles for support.

1. **WITH SKIS IN PARALLEL POSITION, PLANT POLES NEAR TIPS AT EITHER END. FACE SLIGHTLY DOWNHILL.**

2. **SWING TIP OF DOWNHILL SKI FORWARD AND UP TO REST TAIL NEAR UPHILL FOOT.**

3. **USE TAIL OF SKI AS PIVOT POINT TO SWIVEL SKI IN OPPOSITE DIRECTION.**

4. SET UPHILL EDGE OF NEW DOWNHILL SKI AND TRANSFER WEIGHT IN PREPARATION FOR SWINGING UPHILL SKI AROUND TO PARALLEL OPPOSITE SKI.

5. SET UPHILL EDGES OF SKIS. PLACE WEIGHT OVER BOTH SKIS USING POLES FOR SUPPORT.

Getting Up from a Fall

Many times it's rather easy just to get up. Other times it's more difficult.

If you seem to be having more trouble than you think you should, try bringing your skis to a parallel position across the fall line.

Set the uphill edges while you hold both poles together. Place the uphill hand near the baskets. With the opposite hand, grasp the handle of the poles. From this position, it's merely a matter of pulling yourself to an upright position.

Learning to Use a Tow or Lift

Tows and lifts have one aspect in common. All are devices to get you up the slope easily. The *rope tow,* the *T-bar lift* and the *chair lift* comprise the three basic types of tows and lifts.

Regardless of the type of tow or lift, always step or ski in the direction of travel when boarding.

The Rope Tow

Move in line parallel with the rope facing uphill. Bend your knees slightly for balance and to cushion the shock of catching onto the rope.

Extend your left hand in front and your right hand around and in back. Let the rope slide through both hands, then slowly tighten your grip. Take a few short-sliding steps until you begin to move forward and up the slope.

Some rope tows are equipped with support bars. It's merely a matter of getting into parallel position with the rope, grasping the rope and adjusting the support to the lower portion of your back.

1. FACE UPHILL, PARALLEL WITH ROPE. KNEES ARE
   FLEXED SLIGHTLY FOR BALANCE.

2. HAND NEAREST ROPE EXTENDS UPHILL. OPPOSITE
   HAND IS AROUND IN BACK. WITHOUT BACK SUPPORT,
   GRASP ROPE WITH BOTH HANDS.

3. WITH SUPPORT, ADJUST BAR TO LOWER BACK. KEEP
   AT LEAST ONE ARM AND HAND ON ROPE FOR BALANCE.

The T-Bar Lift

Two skiers may use the same T-bar. When getting on the T-bar, face in the direction of travel and look over your inside shoulder. As the T-bar comes to you, grasp the upright on the "T" with your free hand and lean against the crossbar. Do not sit!

Keep your skis parallel and close together. At the top of the hill, one skier pushes away from the T-bar and skis away. The second skier is then free to release and clear the lift.

The Chair Lift

As the name implies, this lift allows you to sit as you go up the slope. Your skis do not touch the snow during the ascent. At some points you may be as many as fifty feet above the surface of the snow.

When getting on the chair lift, ski into position and put the poles in your outer hand. Watch for the chair and steady it with your free hand. Sit in the chair while lifting your ski tips up.

As you get to the top of the hill, place your skis parallel upon the snow, stand up and ski away.

1. SKI INTO POSITION. PLACE POLES IN OUTER HAND.
2. WATCH FOR CHAIR, THEN STEADY IT WITH FREE HAND.

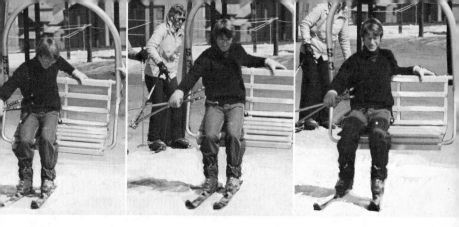

3. SIT IN CHAIR WHILE LIFTING TIPS OF SKIS UPWARD.

4. AT THE TOP, PLACE SKIS IN PARALLEL POSITION UPON SNOW, STAND UP AND SKI AWAY.

Adjusting Your Skiing to Varying Conditions and Terrain

Powder Snow—Skiing powder snow is one of skiing's most breathtaking experiences. Although the opportunity to ski deep powder snow does not present itself often for most skiers, it is well to know what adjustments to make. Generally, it takes some practice to become an accomplished powder snow skier. Because this billowy, frothy snow offers more resistance, maintaining good speed is an important factor. Also, you must hold the front tips of your skis upward to achieve a planing action upon the snow even though the tips of your skis may not be completely visible, if at all.

To plane upon the snow, lean back farther than normal, placing weight over your heels. Knees are bent with feet in a close, parallel position. Allowing the feet to separate breaks down the "planing surface" presented by the skis, often resulting in a spill.

Tracks left in the powder by other skiers also can present some problems. Skiing with good rhythm helps to overcome such obstacles. Rather than sharp right-angle turns from a traverse position, it is better to make continuous turns near the fall line, using smooth, down-unweighting movements.

Packed Snow—A condition more familiar to most skiers. Freshly packed snow provides skiers the opportunity to initiate good skiing technique, to experiment and to practice.

Most major skiing sites are groomed and tailored to provide the average recreational skier with excellent skiing. Generally these areas have slopes of varying difficulty so that beginners and advancd skiers find challenge and enjoyment.

Icy Snow—Edge control is absolutely essential for successful skiing under icy conditions. The sensation of skidding on the icy snow while making turns may be disconcerting indeed. However, with good leg control and forward pressure on the tips of the skis as the turn is completed a reasonably good skiing posture can be maintained.

Once an initial fear of skiing on icy snow is overcome, skiing under such conditions can be rather exhilarating. Most Eastern skiers become quite adept at skiing icy slopes since icy snow is generally more common to the East than to the West. Ice patches are potentially more troublesome than larger areas of ice since many go undetected until it's too late to adjust. Color variations in the snow give the best clue as to where patches of ice lie. Avoid these patches where you can. Where you can't, ski across, then turn once you reach more loosely packed snow. Often the sides of trails are less icy; thus they provide better skiing possibilities under generally icy conditions.

Moguls—Humps of snow which develop on the slope or trail are called moguls. These bumps in the snow build up because almost all other skiers turn in the same spot. Moguls tend to develop in series since skiers ski over the top of one, then turn. Another mogul then develops at that point.

To ski moguls successfully, moderate your speed and bend well at the knees. Use the tops of the moguls as pivot points. As you reach the peak of each hump make your turn, letting your knees absorb the shock of the bump.

With greater speed you may choose to ski the gullies while banking your turn on the sides of each mogul. Moguls can be fun to ski once you have acquired the confidence to handle them.

Flat Light—On very cloudy days shadows are less discernible if existing at all. Tinted yellow goggles usually help give some definition to the terrain. Best advice is to slow down and stay to the side of the trail for a better overview of the slope.

Steep Slopes vs. Gentle Slopes—The natural instinct to lean backward or toward the hill on steep slopes is overcome through experience. Once you gain confidence and start to project your weight forward, your skis begin to work for you. In fact, steep slopes are much easier to ski than gentle or more flat ones. Good pole action and edge control are important factors in skiing the steeper slopes successfully.

Safety Precautions to Remember

• Always check the condition of your equipment before skiing. Make sure everything is in proper working order. Remember, safety bindings have to be adjusted each time you use them.

• Use common sense and good manners. Be careful when carrying your skis.

• Ski with a friend when possible and stay on marked trails. Suit the type of course to your skill level.

• Be courteous at the tows or lifts even though you may have to wait in line. Above all do not "goof off" on the lifts to jeopardize your safety and the safety of others.

• Study the slope, particularly if it is new to you. Ask other skiers about any peculiarities. Observe how other skiers traverse the slope.

• Don't ski in bad weather or try for that last run before dark. Quit skiing when you get tired. When tired, you are prone to make mistakes possibly resulting in an accident.

• Learn your own limits and always use good judgment.

• If you take a spill which seems to injure you, lie still. Get in a comfortable position and wait for help. Most ski areas are well patrolled.

• When you see another skier in distress, stop to help if necessary. Do not try to move the fallen skier. Signal for help and stay with the skier or ski to get help after taking note of surrounding landmarks necessary to locating the skier again.

glossary of skiing terms

ABSTEM: Pushing the tail of the downhill ski downhill from a parallel position with the uphill ski.

ANGULATION: Placing pressure on the uphill edge of the downhill ski by pushing the downhill knee and hip uphill while leaning the upper body downhill to maintain balance. The amount of angulation is related to the slope of the hill.

ANTICIPATION: Turning downhill of the upper body with the pole plant to initiate the turn.

AVALEMENT: Used in turns executed without up-motion or rebound action. *Avalement* is a retracting of the legs and pushing ahead of the feet—an action which is effective in racing turns and for skiing bumpy terrain.

BALANCED POSITION: The body's reacting to maintain balance when the skis accelerate, slow or run at a steady speed.

BOILER PLATE: Ice which results on a hill when a freeze follows a warm period.

CORN SNOW: A type of snow condition caused by alternate freezing and thawing in the spring.

DOWNHILL: In racing, *downhill* is one of the three types of Alpine competition. **Ski:** the *downhill ski* is the lower ski or the ski which will become the downhill ski upon completion of a turn.

EDGING: Angulating to cause the edges of the skis to bite more firmly on the hill.

FLUSH: Slalom gates—three or more in a series which are closed gates.

GIANT SLALOM: One of the three types of Alpine racing which combines the speed of downhill with fewer control gates than for the slalom.

GLM (Graduated Length Method): A method of learning to ski which involves starting the beginning skier on short skis (two to four feet long) and gradually moving the skier to longer skis as the skier progresses in skill until he achieves his final ski length.

HEEL THRUST: Pushing the tails of the skis downhill while releasing the skis' edges.

KICK TURN: A 180-degree change in direction while standing stationary.

MOGUL: Bump on a hill caused by skiing. Steep slopes generally have more and larger ones than do gentle-rolling hills.

POWDER: New dry snow.

ROTATION: A turning of the upper body in the direction of the turn so as to turn the legs when the hips are locked. **Counter Rotation:** A rapid turning of the upper body in the opposite direction of the turn.

"SKI!": A cry of warning when a ski is loose on the hill—similar to the warning of "Fore!" in golf.

SLALOM: One of the three types of Alpine racing. The skier must make a number of turns through a series of gates.

SNOW BUNNY: A beginning skier.

SNOWPLOW: A learning maneuver for controlling speed.

STEM: Spreading the tail of the uphill ski to point the uphill ski downhill while in a traverse.

STEM TURN: Turning by placing weight on the uphill ski the tail of which is spread in a downhill direction.

TRAVERSE: Crossing a slope with the skis parallel.

UNWEIGHTING: Displacing or reducing the skier's weight on the skis to permit maneuvering. *Unweighting* can be accomplished with either a rapid down-motion or up with an up-motion.

WEIGHT TRANSFER: Changing weight from one side to the other.

notes

notes